Sweet
KNITS

9 Baby Projects Sure
To Be Your Favorite

LEISURE ARTS, INC. • Maumelle, Arkansas

Contents

Cuddle Bear Blankie

●●○○ **EASY**

SIZE

About 18 in. (45.5 cm) long

GAUGE

13 sts = about 4 in. (10 cm) in Garter st (k every st on every row).

BE SURE TO CHECK YOUR GAUGE.

MATERIALS

Yarn (Bulky)
Lion Brand® BABY SOFT® BOUCLE (Art. #918)

- ☐ #150 Cloud 1 ball (A)
- ☐ #100 White 1 ball (B)
- ☐ Lion Brand® knitting needles size 8 (5 mm)
- ☐ Lion Brand® stitch markers
- ☐ Lion Brand® large-eyed blunt needle

Additional Materials

Small amount of black yarn for face

Small amount of fiberfill stuffing

NOTES

1. Blankie is worked in one piece, beginning at one corner, with 2 colors of yarn.

2. The bear head is seamed and then stuffed, the eyes and nose are embroidered onto the head.

3. The ears are created by simply sewing across the head.

4. Stitches for the paws are picked up along sides of Blankie.

STITCH EXPLANATIONS

kfb (knit in front and back)

An increase worked as follows:

1. Knit the next st through the front loop, but do not remove the st from your left hand needle.

2. Knit the same st once more, this time inserting your needle through the back loop of the st. You will have created 2 loops (sts) on your right hand needle.

3. Drop the st from your left hand needle – you have increased 1 st.

BLANKIE

With A, cast on 3 sts.

Row 1: K1, kfb, k1 – you'll have 4 sts.

Row 2: K2, kfb, knit to end of row.

Repeat Row 2 until you have 22 sts.

On the next row, you'll begin a two color stripe pattern. No need to cut yarn between color changes, just carry the yarn color you're not using along the side edge of the Blankie.

Blankie Stripe pattern

With B, rep Row 2 for 4 times – 26 sts .

Continue to rep Row 2, working 4 rows with A and 4 rows with B alternately, until you have 50 sts. You should be on the last row of a B stripe.

Change to A and knit 4 rows. Place a st marker on each end of this stripe for paw placement.

Change to B.

Next Row: K2, k2tog, knit to end of row.

With B, rep last row 3 more times.

Repeat last row, working 4 rows with A and 4 rows with B alternately, until you have 28 sts. Your last row should be the second row of an A stripe.

Shape Head

Next row: With B, k2tog across – you'll have 14 sts.

Next row: With B, k2, kfb, k to last 3 sts, kfb, k2 – 16 sts.

Change to A and knit 2 rows.

Change to B and knit 2 rows.

Repeat last 4 rows 3 more times.

Change to A and knit 4 rows – this stripe is the top of the head.

Change to B and knit 2 rows.

Change to A and knit 2 rows.

Repeat last 4 rows 3 more times.

Change to B and knit 2 rows.

Bind off and cut yarn, leaving a long yarn tail.

Fold head in half across top of head stripe.

With B yarn tail threaded into blunt needle, sew through both layers across bound off edge, sewing back of head to front.

Sew long straight sts through both layers across 'neck', then pull to gather neck. Knot and fasten off.

With B, sew one side of head closed. Sew a diagonal line of straight sts across each side of head, through both layers, to make ears.

Stuff head with a small amount of fiberfill, then sew remaining side of head closed.

Paws

With A, pick up and k7 sts along the marked A stripe on Blankie.

Knit one row with A.

Change to B and knit 2 rows.

Knit 2 rows with A, then 2 rows with B.

Repeat last 4 rows once more.

Cut B and continue with A only.

With A, knit 12 rows.

Bind off.

Repeat on opposite side of Blankie to make a second paw. Knot end of each paw.

FINISHING

With black yarn threaded into blunt needle, embroider straight stitch eyes and nose.

Weave in ends.

Gowanus
Baby Wrap Cardi

●●○○ **EASY**

SIZES

1 year (2 years, 3 years)

Finished Chest:
About 21 (23, 25) in.
[53.5 (58.5, 63.5) cm]

Finished Length:
About 10½ (11½, 12½) in.
[26.5 (29, 32) cm]

Note: Pattern is written for smallest size with changes for larger sizes in parentheses. When only one number is given, it applies to all sizes. To follow pattern more easily, circle all numbers pertaining to your size before beginning.

GAUGE

20 sts + 28 rows = about 4 in. (10 cm) in St st (k on RS, p on WS).
BE SURE TO CHECK YOUR GAUGE.

MATERIALS

Yarn (Medium)
   Lion Brand® FEELS LIKE BUTTA (Art. #215)

☐ #101 Pink 2 (3, 3) balls

☐ Lion Brand® knitting needles size 7 (4.5 mm)

☐ Lion Brand® stitch markers

☐ Lion Brand® stitch holders

☐ Lion Brand® large-eyed blunt needle

Additional Materials
Spare knitting needle size 7 (4.5 mm) for 3-Needle Bind-off

NOTES

1. Cardi is made in 5 pieces: Back, Left and Right Front, and 2 Sleeves.

2. Shoulders are joined with 3-Needle Bind-off.

3. Ties are worked separately and sewn to Cardi.

STITCH EXPLANATIONS

kfb (knit in front and back)
Knit next st without removing it from left needle, then knit through back of same st – 1 st increased.

ssk (slip, slip, knit) Slip next 2 sts as if to knit, one at a time, to right needle; insert left needle into fronts of these 2 sts and knit them tog – 1 st decreased.

BACK
Cast on 52 (57, 62) sts.

Work in Garter st (k every st on every row) for 3 rows.

Beg with a RS (knit) row, work in St st (k on RS, p on WS) until piece measures about 10 (11, 12) in. **[25.5 (28, 30.5) cm]** from beg, end with a RS row as the last row you work.

Shoulders and Back Neck
Row 1 (WS): P16 (18, 20) for left shoulder, k20 (21, 22) for back neck, p16 (18, 20) for right shoulder.

Row 2: Knit.

Row 3: Rep Row 1.

Row 4: K16 (18, 20) and place these sts on a holder for left shoulder, bind off next 20 (21, 22) sts for back neck, k to end and place these sts on a holder for right shoulder.

LEFT FRONT
Cast on 49 (54, 59) sts.

Work in Garter st (k every st on every row) for 3 rows.

Next Row (RS): Knit.

Next Row: K3 for Garter st neck edge, p to end of row.

Rep last 2 rows until piece measures about 5½ (6, 6½) in. **[14 (15, 16.5) cm]** from beg, end with a WS row as the last row you work.

Shape Neck
Row 1 (RS): K to last 5 sts, k2tog, k3 – you will have 48 (53, 58) sts in this row.

Row 2: K3, p2tog, p to end of row – 47 (52, 57) sts.

Rep Rows 1 and 2 until 16 (18, 20) sts rem.

....

NOTE: For sizes 1 and 3 years, your last row will be a RS row; for size 2 years, your last row will be a WS row.

....

Keeping 3 neck edge sts in Garter st and rem sts in St st, work even until piece measures same as Back, end with a RS row as the last row you work.

Place rem 16 (18, 20) sts on a holder.

RIGHT FRONT
Cast on 49 (54, 59) sts.

Work in Garter st (k every st on every row) for 3 rows.

Next Row (RS): Knit.

Next Row: P to last 3 sts, k3 for Garter st neck edge.

Rep last 2 rows until piece measures about 5½ (6, 6½) in. **[14 (15, 16.5) cm]** from beg, end with a WS row as the last row you work.

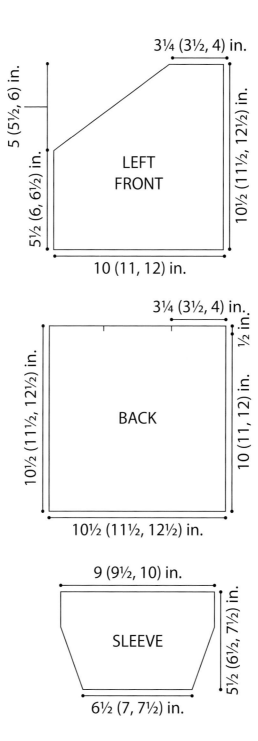

LEFT FRONT

3¼ (3½, 4) in.

5 (5½, 6) in.

5½ (6, 6½) in.

10½ (11½, 12½) in.

10 (11, 12) in.

BACK

3¼ (3½, 4) in.

½ in.

10½ (11½, 12½) in.

10 (11, 12) in.

10½ (11½, 12½) in.

SLEEVE

9 (9½, 10) in.

5½ (6½, 7½) in.

6½ (7, 7½) in.

Shape Neck

Row 1 (RS): K3, ssk, k to end of row – you will have 48 (53, 58) sts in this row.

Row 2: P to last 5 sts, p2tog, k3 – 47 (52, 57) sts.

Rep Rows 1 and 2 until 16 (18, 20) sts rem.

Keeping 3 neck edge sts in Garter st and rem sts in St st, work even until piece measures same as Back, end with a RS row as the last row you work.

Place rem 16 (18, 20) sts on a holder.

SLEEVES *(Make 2)*

Cast on 32 (35, 38) sts.

Work in Garter st (k every st on every row) for 3 rows.

Next Row (RS): K1, kfb, k to last 2 sts, kfb, k1 – 34 (37, 40) sts.

Work even in St st for 3 rows.

Rep last 4 rows until you have 44 (47, 50) sts.

Work even in St st until piece measures about 5½ (6½, 7½) in. [14 (16.5, 19) cm] from beg.

Bind off.

LEFT TIE

Cast on 63 sts.

Knit 1 row.

Bind off.

RIGHT TIE

Cast on 110 (120, 130) sts.

Knit 1 row.

Bind off.

FINISHING

Place left front shoulder sts from holder onto one needle and left back shoulder sts from holder onto a second needle. Join left shoulder using 3-Needle Bind-off, as follows:

With RS of shoulders together, hold the 2 needles in one hand. With 3rd needle, knit tog 1 st from each needle, *knit tog 1 st from each needle, pass first st worked over 2nd to bind off; rep from * across.

Cut yarn and pull through last st to secure.

Join right shoulder using 3-Needle Bind-off in the same way.

Place markers on Fronts and Back, about 4½ (4¾, 5) in. [11.5 (12, 12.5) cm] down from shoulder seams. Sew Sleeves between markers.

Sew Sleeve seams. Sew side seams leaving ½ in. (1.5 cm) unsewn on left side seam about 5½ (6, 6½) in. [14 (15, 16.5) cm] from lower edge for Tie opening.

Sew Ties to Fronts at beg of neck shaping.

Weave in ends.

Glenwood Child's Cardigan

●●○○ **EASY**

SIZES

Child's XS (S, M, L, XL)

Finished Chest:
About 23 (25, 28, 32, 34) in.
[58.5 (63.5, 71, 81.5, 86.5) cm]

Finished Length:
About 13½ (14½, 16, 19½, 22) in.
[34.5 (37, 40.5, 49.5, 56) cm]

Note: Pattern is written for smallest size with changes for larger sizes in parentheses. When only one number is given, it applies to all sizes. To follow pattern more easily, circle all numbers pertaining to your size before beginning.

GAUGE

16 sts + 22 rows = about 4 in. (10 cm) in St st (k on RS, p on WS).
BE SURE TO CHECK YOUR GAUGE.

MATERIALS

Yarn (Medium)
LION BRAND® FEELS LIKE BUTTA BONUS BUNDLE® (Art. #123)

☐ #108 Dusty Blue 1 (1, 2, 2, 3) balls

☐ LION BRAND® knitting needles size 9 (5.5 mm)

☐ LION BRAND® stitch markers

☐ LION BRAND® large-eyed blunt needle

Additional Materials

Circular knitting needle size 9 (5.5 mm), 36 in. (91.5 cm) long

4 (4, 5, 5, 6) buttons, about ½ in. (13 mm) diameter

NOTES

1. Cardigan is worked in 5 pieces – Back, Left and Right Fronts and 2 Sleeves.

2. Lower edge of Cardigan and Sleeves are worked in Garter st.

3. Stitches for front bands are picked up around edges of Cardigan, then worked in Garter st.

STITCH EXPLANATIONS

M1 (make 1) An increase worked by lifting the horizontal thread lying between the needles and placing it onto left needle. Knit this new stitch through the back loop.

ssk (slip, slip, knit) Slip next 2 sts as if to knit, one at a time, to right needle; insert left needle into fronts of these 2 sts and knit them tog – 1 st decreased.

Yo (yarn over)

An increase that also creates a small decorative hole (eyelet) in the fabric, worked as follows:

1. Bring yarn to front, between the needles.

2. Take yarn to back, over the right needle. This creates the new st. You are now ready to proceed with the next st as instructed.

BACK

With straight needles, cast on 46 (52, 56, 64, 68) sts.

Work in Garter st (k every st on every row) for 7 (11, 15, 15, 19) rows.

Beg with a WS (purl) row, work in St st (k on RS, p on WS) until piece measures about 8½ (9, 10, 13, 15) in. **[**21.5 (23, 25.5, 33, 38) cm**]** from beg, end with a WS row as the last row you work.

Shape Armholes

Next Row (RS): Bind off 4 sts, k to end of row – 42 (48, 52, 60, 64) sts.

Next Row: Bind off 4 sts, p to end of row – 38 (44, 48, 56, 60) sts at the end of this row.

Work even in St st until piece measures about 13½ (14½, 16, 19½, 22) in. **[**34.5 (37, 40.5, 49.5, 56) cm**]** from beg.

Bind off.

LEFT FRONT

With straight needles, cast on 22 (24, 26, 30, 32) sts.

Work in Garter st for 7 (11, 15, 15, 19) rows.

Beg with a WS (purl) row, work in St st until piece measures same length as Back to armholes, end with a WS row as the last row you work.

Shape Armhole and Neck

Next Row (RS): Bind off 4 sts, k to last 3 sts, k2tog, k1 – 17 (19, 21, 25, 27) sts at the end of this row.

Next Row: Purl.

Dec Row for Neck (RS): K to last 3 sts, k2tog, k1 – 16 (18, 20, 24, 26) sts.

Next Row: Purl.

Rep last 2 rows 7 (6, 5, 8, 7) more times – 9 (12, 15, 16, 19) sts rem after all decs have been completed.

Next Row (RS): Rep Dec Row for Neck – 8 (11, 14, 15, 18) sts.

Work in St st for 3 rows.

NOTE: When you see '0' reps in the instructions, this means that for your specific size, you need not rep anything, simply continue to the next section of the instructions.

Rep last 4 rows 0 (1, 2, 1, 2) more time(s) – 8 (10, 12, 14, 16) sts.

Rep Dec Row for Neck – 7 (9, 11, 13, 15) sts.

Work even in St st until piece measures same length as Back.

Bind off.

RIGHT FRONT

Cast on and work as for Left Front to Shape Armhole, but end with a RS row as the last row you work.

Shape Armhole and Neck

Next Row (WS): Bind off 4 sts, p to end of row – 18 (20, 22, 26, 28) sts.

Dec Row for Neck (RS): K1, ssk, k to end of row – 17 (19, 21, 25, 27) sts.

Next Row: Purl.

Rep last 2 rows 8 (7, 6, 9, 8) more times – 9 (12, 15, 16, 19) sts rem after all decs have been completed.

Next Row (RS): Rep Dec Row for Neck – 8 (11, 14, 15, 18) sts.

Work in St st for 3 rows.

Rep last 4 rows 0 (1, 2, 1, 2) more time(s) – 8 (10, 12, 14, 16) sts.

Rep Dec Row for Neck – 7 (9, 11, 13, 15) sts.

Work even in St st until piece measures same length as Back.

Bind off.

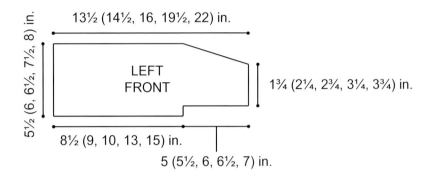

13½ (14½, 16, 19½, 22) in.

5½ (6, 6½, 7½, 8) in.

LEFT FRONT

1¾ (2¼, 2¾, 3¼, 3¾) in.

8½ (9, 10, 13, 15) in.

5 (5½, 6, 6½, 7) in.

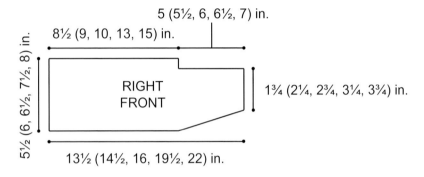

5 (5½, 6, 6½, 7) in.

8½ (9, 10, 13, 15) in.

5½ (6, 6½, 7½, 8) in.

RIGHT FRONT

1¾ (2¼, 2¾, 3¼, 3¾) in.

13½ (14½, 16, 19½, 22) in.

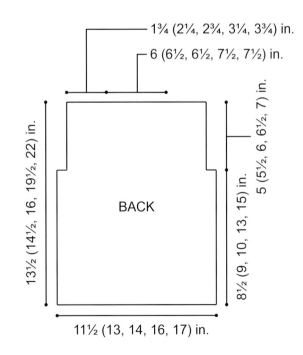

1¾ (2¼, 2¾, 3¼, 3¾) in.

6 (6½, 6½, 7½, 7½) in.

13½ (14½, 16, 19½, 22) in.

5 (5½, 6, 6½, 7) in.

BACK

8½ (9, 10, 13, 15) in.

11½ (13, 14, 16, 17) in.

SLEEVES *(Make 2)*

With straight needles, cast on 22 (24, 26, 28, 30) sts.

Work in Garter st for 7 (11, 15, 15, 19) rows.

Beginning with a WS (purl) row, work in St st for 3 rows.

Next (Inc) Row (RS): K1, M1, k to last st, M1, k1 – 24 (26, 28, 30, 32) sts at the end of this row.

Continue in St st, AND AT THE SAME TIME, rep last Inc Row every 4th row 8 (1, 3, 0, 0) more time(s), then every 6th row 0 (8, 7, 11, 12) times – 40 (44, 48, 52, 56) sts after all incs have been completed.

Work even (without further increasing) in St st until piece measures about 9 (13½, 14½, 17, 18½) in. **[**23 (34.5, 37, 43, 47) cm**]** from beg.

Bind off.

FINISHING

Sew shoulder seams.

Neck and Front Bands

Place markers for 4 (4, 5, 5, 6) buttonholes evenly spaced along right front edge for girl's Cardigan or along left front edge for boy's Cardigan.

From RS, with circular needle, pick up and k31 (33, 37, 48, 56) sts evenly spaced along front edge of Right Front, 21 (23, 25, 27, 29) sts along right front neck, 18 (20, 22, 24, 24) sts across back neck, 21 (23, 25, 27, 29) sts along left front neck, and 31 (33, 37, 48, 56) sts along front edge of Left Front – 122 (132, 146, 174, 194) sts.

Working back and forth on circular needle as if working on straight needles, work in Garter st for 2 (2, 2, 3, 3) rows.

NOTE: After working a few rows, you may decide that your band would look better if you had picked up more or fewer sts than the amount indicated for your size. Since a well-balanced band adds a beautiful finishing touch to your Cardigan, we strongly recommend that if you've any doubts, simply pull out the sts and adjust the number that you pick up. The pattern instruction reflects the number that the designer picked up – but everyone's knitting is a bit different.

Next Row: Knit, working (k2tog, yo) at each marker to make buttonholes.

Continue in Garter st for (2, 2, 3, 3) more rows.

Bind off.

Sew in Sleeves. Sew side and Sleeve seams.

Sew buttons to buttonband opposite buttonholes.

Weave in ends.

LION BRAND® BABYSOFT®

Rock The Casbah Afghan

●●○○ **EASY**

SIZE

About 36 x 36 in. (91.5 x 91.5 cm)

GAUGE

1 ripple = about 3 in. (7.5 cm)
measured from peak to peak.
BE SURE TO CHECK YOUR GAUGE.

MATERIALS

Yarn (Light)
Lion Brand® BABYSOFT®
(Art. #920)

☐ #136 Apricot 1 ball (A)

☐ #107 Bluebell 1 ball (B)

☐ #192 Orchid 1 ball (C)

☐ #178 Teal 1 ball (D)

☐ Lion Brand® large-eyed
blunt needle

Additional Materials
Circular knitting needle size 6
(4 mm), 29 in. (73.5 cm) long

NOTES

1. Afghan is worked in one piece in an easy ripple pattern.

2. A circular needle is used to accommodate the large number of sts.
   Work back and forth in rows as if working with straight needles.

3. Yarn color is changed following a Stripe Sequence to make stripes.

4. To slip the first stitch of each row, you can slip as if to knit or slip
   as if to purl, whichever looks best with your knitting style.

STITCH EXPLANATIONS

kfb (knit in front and back) Knit next st without removing it from left hand needle, then k through back of same st – 1 st increased.

ssk (slip, slip, knit) Slip next 2 sts as if to knit, one at a time, to right hand needle; insert left hand needle into fronts of these 2 sts and knit them tog – 1 st decreased.

AFGHAN

With A, cast on 246 sts.

Row 1: Sl 1, k2, *kfb, k7, ssk, k2tog, k7, kfb; rep from * to last 3 sts, k2, p1 – you will have 12 ripples.

Row 2: Sl 1, k to last st, p1.

Rep Rows 1 and 2 changing color as in following Stripe Sequence: Work 4 more rows with A, 6 rows with B, 6 rows with C, 6 rows with D, 30 rows with A, 6 rows with B, 6 rows with C, 6 rows with D, 6 rows with A, 30 rows with B, 6 rows with C, 6 rows with D, 6 rows with A, 6 rows with B, 30 rows with C, 6 rows with D, 6 rows with A, 6 rows with B, 6 rows with C, 30 rows with D, 6 rows with A, 6 rows with B, 6 rows with C, and 6 rows with D.

With D, bind off.

FINISHING

Weave in ends.

Diagonal Baby Afghan

●●○○ **EASY**

SIZE

About 30 x 30 in. (76 x 76 cm)

GAUGE

13 sts = about 4 in. (10 cm) in Garter st (knit every st on every row).

BE SURE TO CHECK YOUR GAUGE.

MATERIALS

Yarn (Bulky)

LION BRAND® BABY SOFT® BOUCLE (Art. #918)

☐ #105 Aqua 5 balls

☐ LION BRAND® large-eyed blunt needle

Additional Materials

Circular knitting needle size 10½ (6.5 mm), 36 in. (91.5 cm) long

NOTES

1. Afghan is worked in one piece on a circular needle.

2. The circular needle is used to accommodate the number of stitches. Work back and forth in rows on the circular needle, just as if working on straight needles.

3. The Afghan is worked diagonally, from corner to corner, and shaped with increases and decreases.

STITCH EXPLANATION

Yo (yarn over)

An increase that also creates a small decorative hole (eyelet) in the fabric, worked as follows:

1. Bring yarn to front, between the needles.

2. Take yarn to back, over the right hand needle. This creates the new st. You are now ready to proceed with the next st as instructed.

AFGHAN

Cast on 5 sts.

Row 1: Knit.

Row 2: K3, yo, k2 – you will have 6 sts.

Row 3: K3, yo, k3 – 7 sts.

Row 4: K3, yo, k to end of row.

Repeat Row 4 until you have 144 sts on your needle.

Next (Decrease) Row: K2, k2tog, yo, k2tog, k to end of row.

Repeat last row until 6 sts remain.

Last Row: K2, k2tog, yo, k2tog – 5 sts.

Bind off remaining 5 sts.

FINISHING

Weave in ends.

26

Branford
Baby Blanket

●●○○ **EASY**

SIZE

About 28 x 30 in. (71 x 76 cm)

GAUGE

14 sts = about 4 in. (10 cm)
over pattern Rows 2 and 3.
BE SURE TO CHECK YOUR GAUGE.

MATERIALS

Yarn (Medium)

LION BRAND® FEELS LIKE
BUTTA BONUS BUNDLE
(Art. #123)

☐ #106 Ice 1 ball

☐ LION BRAND® stitch markers

☐ LION BRAND® large-eyed
blunt needle

Additional Materials

Circular knitting needle size 8
(5 mm), 36 in. (91.5 cm) long

NOTES

1. Blanket is worked in one piece on a circular needle.

2. The circular needle is used to accommodate the large number of sts.
    Work back and forth in rows on the circular needle, just as if working
    on straight needles.

3. The Blanket has a Garter stitch border on all sides. The border is
    worked in with the Blanket.

BLANKET

Cast on 100 sts.

Beginning Border

Work in Garter st (knit every st on every row) for 12 rows.

Pattern Rows

Row 1: K6 and place a marker, p4, *k2, p4; repeat from * to last 6 sts, place a marker, k to end of row.

Row 2: Knit across the row, slipping markers as you come to them.

Row 3: K6, slip marker, p4, *k2, p4; repeat from * to last 6 sts, slip marker, k to end of row.

Repeat Rows 2 and 3 until piece measures about 28½ in. (72.5 cm) from beginning, end with Row 3 as the last row you work.

Ending Border

Next Row: Knit, removing markers as you come to them.

Work in Garter st for 11 rows.

Bind off all sts.

FINISHING

Weave in ends.

Simple Diagonal Baby Afghan

●○○○ **BASIC**

SIZE

About 32 x 32 in. (81.5 x 81.5 cm)

GAUGE

13 sts = about 4 in. (10 cm)
in Garter st (knit every stitch on
every row) with one strand each
of A and B held together.
BE SURE TO CHECK YOUR GAUGE.

MATERIALS LIGHT

Yarn (Light) **3**
LION BRAND® ICE CREAM®
(Art. #923)

☐ #206 Tutti Frutti 2 balls (A)

☐ #201 Cotton Candy 2 balls (B)

☐ LION BRAND® circular
knitting needle size 10½
(6.5 mm), 29 in. (73.5 cm) long

☐ LION BRAND® large-eyed
blunt needle

NOTES

1. Afghan is worked in Garter st (knit every stitch on every row)
   from corner to corner with 2 strands of yarn held together. The
   first half of the Afghan is shaped with yarn over increases and the
   second half is shaped with decreases.

2. A circular needle is used to accommodate the large number of stitches.
   Work back and forth in rows on the circular needle as if knitting with
   straight needles.

STITCH EXPLANATION

Yo (yarn over)

An increase that also creates a small decorative hole (eyelet) in the fabric, worked as follows:

1. Bring yarn to front, between the needles.

2. Take yarn to back, over the right hand needle. This creates the new st. You are now ready to proceed with the next st as instructed.

AFGHAN

With one strand each of A and B held together, cast on 5 sts.

Increase Half

Row 1: Knit.

Row 2: K3, yo, k2 – 6 sts.

Row 3: K3, yo, k3 – 7 sts.

Row 4: K3, yo, k to end of row – 8 sts.

Repeat Row 4 until you have 140 sts.

Decrease Half

Next Row (Decrease Row): K2, k2tog, yo, k2tog, k to end of row – 139 sts.

Repeat last row until 5 sts remain.

Bind off.

FINISHING

Weave in ends.

Bonaire
Baby Blankie

■■ □□ **EASY**

SIZE

About 32 x 32 in. (81.5 x 81.5 cm)

GAUGE

17 sts + 34 rows = about 4 in. (10 cm) in Garter st (knit every st on every row).

1 Strip = about 8 in. (20.5 cm) wide.

BE SURE TO CHECK YOUR GAUGE.

MATERIALS

Yarn (Medium)
Lion Brand® FEELS LIKE BUTTA (Art. #215)

☐ #158 Lemon 2 balls (A)

☐ #146 Lilac 2 balls (B)

☐ #156 Mint 2 balls (C)

☐ #101 Pink 2 balls (D)

☐ Lion Brand® knitting needles size 7 (4.5 mm)

☐ Lion Brand® large-eyed blunt needle

NOTES

1. Four Strips are worked separately, then sewn together to make the Blankie.

2. Each Strip is worked with 4 colors of yarn to create a patchwork block effect.

STRIP I

With A, cast on 34 sts.

With A, work in Garter st (knit every st on every row) until piece measures about 8 in. (20.5 cm) from beginning.

Change to B.

With B, knit. Mark this row as the right side of the Blankie.

Continue in Garter st with B until B block of color measures about 8 in. (20.5 cm), be sure to end with a wrong side row as the last row you work.

Change to C, and continue in Garter st until C block of color measures about 8 in. (20.5 cm), again ending with a wrong side row as the last row you work.

Change to D and continue in Garter st until D block of color measures about 8 in. (20.5 cm).

Bind off.

STRIP II

Make same as Strip I, using colors in this order: B, C, D and A.

STRIP III

Make same as Strip I, using colors in this order: C, D, A and B.

STRIP IV

Make same as Strip I, using colors in this order: D, A, B and C.

FINISHING

Following the diagram, sew long edges of Strips together.

Weave in ends.

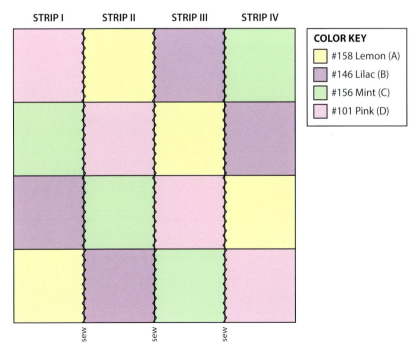

COLOR KEY
- #158 Lemon (A)
- #146 Lilac (B)
- #156 Mint (C)
- #101 Pink (D)

LION BRAND® ICE CREAM

Sugar and Spice Shorts Set

●●○○ **EASY**

SIZES

To fit 1 year (2 years, 3 years)

Top

Circumference at Chest:
About 22 (23, 24) in.
[56 (58.5, 61) cm]

Finished Length:
About 12½ (14½, 16) in.
[32 (37, 40.5) cm]

Shorts

Finished Waist:
About 26 (28, 29) in.
[66 (71, 73.5) cm], without elastic

Finished Length:
About 7½ (9, 10) in.
[19 (23, 25.5) cm}

Note: Pattern is written for smallest size with changes for larger sizes in parentheses. When only one number is given, it applies to all sizes. To follow pattern more easily, circle all numbers pertaining to your size before beginning.

GAUGE

21 sts + 28 rows = 4 in. (10 cm) in St st (k on RS, p on WS) with larger needles and A.
BE SURE TO CHECK YOUR GAUGE.

MATERIALS

Yarn (Light) **3**
Lion Brand® ICE CREAM (Art. #923)

- ☐ #206 Tutti Frutti 1 (2, 2) balls (A)
- ☐ #306 Rainbow 1 (2, 2) balls (B)
- ☐ Lion Brand® knitting needles size 6 (4 mm)
- ☐ Lion Brand® stitch markers
- ☐ Lion Brand® stitch holders
- ☐ Lion Brand® large-eyed blunt needle

Additional Materials

Circular knitting needle size 5 (3.75 mm), 24 in. (61 cm) long

24 in. (61 cm) elastic, 1 in. (2.5 cm) wide

Sewing needle and thread

One small button

NOTES

1. Top is worked in 2 pieces – Back and Front.

2. Decreases are worked on Top to create a cute A-line shape.

3. A slit is made at center Back so the Top will fit easily over baby's head!

4. Garter st (k every st on every row) edging is worked around neck and armholes of Top.

5. Legs of Shorts are worked separately, then joined to work the waistband.

6. Waistband is folded to make a casing for the elastic – waist size can be adjusted by cutting the elastic to the correct length.

7. End with a WS row means that the last row you work should be a WS row, and the next row that you are ready to work will be a RS row.

8. When you see '– 12 sts' in the instructions, this lets you know how many sts you will have at the end of that specific row.

TOP

FRONT

With straight needles and A, cast on 68 (70, 74) sts.

Rows 1-8: Knit.

Row 9 (Decrease Row) (RS): K4, k2tog, k to last 6 stitches, k2tog, k to end of row – you will have 66 (68, 72) sts at the end of this row.

Rows 10-16: Beg with a WS (purl) row, work in St st (k on RS, p on WS).

Rows 17-40: Rep Rows 9-16 for 3 more times – 60 (62, 66) sts when all rows have been worked.

Row 41: Rep Row 9 – 58 (60, 64) sts.

Continue in St st until piece measures about 8 (9, 10) in. **[20.5 (23, 25.5) cm]** from beg, end with a WS row as the last row you work.

Shape Armholes

Row 1 (RS): Bind off 4 sts, k to end of row – 54 (56, 60) sts.

Row 2: Bind off 4 sts, p to end of row – 50 (52, 56) sts.

Row 3 (Decrease Row): K1, k2tog, k to last 3 sts, k2tog, K1 – 48 (50, 54) sts.

Row 4: Purl.

Rep Rows 3 and 4 for 3 (3, 4) more times – 42 (44, 46) sts when all decreases have been completed.

Continue in St st for 2 rows.

Rep Row 3 – 40 (42, 44) sts.

Continue in St st until armholes measure about 2½ (3½, 4) in. **[6.5 (9, 10) cm]**, end with a WS row as the last row you work.

Shape Neck

NOTE: You'll be shaping one side of the front neck at a time.

First Shoulder

Row 1 (RS): K15 (16, 16) and sl these sts onto a st holder for second side, bind off 10 (10, 12) sts, k to end of row – 15 (16, 16) sts rem.

Rows 2, 4, 6 and 8: Purl.

Row 3: Bind off 3 sts, k to end of row – 12 (13, 13) sts.

Row 5: Bind off 2 sts, k to end of row – 10 (11, 11) sts.

Row 7: K2tog, k to end of row – 9 (10, 10) sts.

Row 9: K2tog, k to end of row – 8 (9, 9) sts.

Rows 10-13: Work in St st.

Bind off.

Second Shoulder

Return 15 (16, 16) sts from st holder to needles so you are ready to work a WS row.

Row 1(WS): Bind off 3 sts, purl to end of row – 12 (13, 13) sts.

Rows 2, 4 and 6: Knit.

Row 3: Bind off 2 sts, p to end of row – 10 (11, 11) sts.

Row 5: P2tog, p to end of row – 9 (10, 10) sts.

Row 7: Rep Row 5 – 8 (9, 9) sts.

Rows 8-11: Work in St st.

Bind off.

BACK

Cast on and work same as Front until armholes measure about 1½ (2½, 3) in. **[**4 (6.5, 7.5) cm**]**, end with a WS row as the last row you work.

Divide for Back Slit
First Shoulder

Next Row (RS): K 20 (21, 22); sl rem sts to a st holder for second side – 20 (21, 22) sts rem for first shoulder.

Continue in St st until armhole measures about 3½ (4½, 5) in. **[**9 (11.5, 12.5) cm**]**, end with a RS row as the last row you work.

Shape Neck

Next Row (WS): Bind off 10 (10, 11) sts, p to end of row – 10 (11, 11) sts.

Next Row: K to last 2 sts, k2tog – 9 (10, 10) sts.

Next Row: Purl.

Next Row: K to last 2 sts, k2tog – 8 (9, 9) sts.

Continue in St st for 4 rows.

Bind off.

Second Shoulder

Return 20 (21, 22) sts from holder to needles so you are ready to work a RS row.

Continue in St st until armhole measures same as first shoulder to neck, end with a WS row as the last row you work.

Shape Neck

Next Row (RS): Bind off 10 (10, 11) sts, k to end of row – 10 (11, 11) sts.

Next Row: Purl.

Next Row: K2tog, k to last end of row – 9 (10, 10) sts.

Next Row: Purl.

Next Row: K2tog, k to last end of row – 8 (9, 9) sts.

Continue in St st for 4 rows.

Bind off.

FINISHING
Sew shoulder seams.

Neck Edging
From RS with circular needle and A, and beg at left Back slit, pick up and k 70 (70, 74) sts evenly spaced around neck edge, ending at right Back slit.

Working back and forth in rows on circular needle as if working on straight needles, knit 2 rows.

Bind off.

Armhole Edging
From RS with circular needle and A, and beg at underarm, pick up and k 52 (62, 68) sts evenly spaced around armhole edge.

Work as for neck edging.

Bind off.

Rep edging on opposite armhole.

Sew side seams, including armhole edging.

Sew button to top of one side of Back slit. Button the Top by inserting the button through the knit fabric.

Weave in ends.

SHORTS

NOTE: Legs are worked separately beg at the lower edge. The waistband is then worked in one piece across the top of both legs.

FIRST LEG
With straight needles and B, cast on 84 (90, 94) sts.

Knit 5 rows.

Beg with a RS (knit) row, work in St st for 10 (14, 18) rows.

Shape Crotch
Next Row (RS): Bind off 4 (4, 5) sts, k to end of row – you will have 80 (86, 89) sts at the end of this row.

Next Row: Bind off 4 (4, 5) sts, p to end of row – 76 (82, 84) sts.

Next Row: K1, k2tog, k to end of row – 75 (81, 83) sts.

Next Row: P1, p2tog, p to end of row – 74 (80, 82) sts.

Rep last 2 rows until 70 (74, 76) sts rem.

Continue in St st until piece measures about 4½ (5, 5½) in. **[**11.5 (12.5, 14) cm**]** from beg of crotch shaping, end with a WS row as the last row you work.

Cut yarn and slip sts for First Leg onto a st holder.

SECOND LEG

Cast on and work same as for First Leg, but do NOT place sts onto a st holder.

Waistband

Next Row (RS): With circular needle and continuing with A, knit across sts of Second Leg, then knit across sts of First Leg from st holder – 140 (148, 152) sts.

Place a marker for beg of rnd and join by working the first st on the left hand needle with the working yarn from the right hand needle.

Rnds 1-7: Knit.

Rnd 8: Purl to make a turning ridge.

Rnds 9-16: Knit.

Bind off.

FINISHING

Sew leg and crotch seams. Fold waistband to WS along turning ridge to make casing and sew in place, leaving an opening to insert elastic. Cut elastic to waist size, then thread through casing.

....

TIP: Attach a large safety pin to one end of the elastic to make threading easier. With sewing needle and thread, seam ends of elastic. Sew opening in casing closed.

....

Weave in ends.

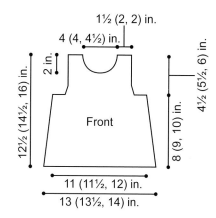

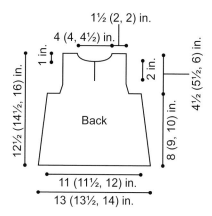

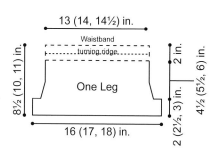

General Instructions

ABBREVIATIONS

beg	begin(ning)
cm	centimeters
dec(s)	decrease(s)
inc	increase(s)
K	knit
K2tog	knit 2 together
K3tog	knit 3 together
kfb	knit front and back
M1	make one
mm	millimeters
P	purl
P2tog	purl 2 together
rem	remain(ing)
rep	repeat
Rnd(s)	Round(s)
RS	right side
sl	slip
SSK	slip, slip, knit
St st	Stockinette stitch
st(s)	stitch(es)
tog	together
YO	yarn over
WS	wrong side
YO	yarn over

KNIT TERMINOLOGY

UNITED STATES	INTERNATIONAL
gauge =	tension
bind off =	cast off
yarn over (YO) =	yarn forward (yfwd) **or** yarn around needle (yrn)

KNITTING NEEDLES

UNITED STATES	ENGLISH U.K.	METRIC (mm)
0	13	2
1	12	2.25
2	11	2.75
3	10	3.25
4	9	3.5
5	8	3.75
6	7	4
7	6	4.5
8	5	5
9	4	5.5
10	3	6
10½	2	6.5
11	1	8
13	00	9
15	000	10
17	---	12.75
19	---	15
35	---	19
50	---	25

●○○○ **BASIC**	Projects using basic stitches. May include basic increases and decreases.
●●○○ **EASY**	Projects may include simple stitch patterns, color work, and/or shaping.
●●●○ **INTERMEDIATE**	Projects may include involved stitch patterns, color work, and/or shaping.
●●●● **COMPLEX**	Projects may include complex stitch patterns, color work, and/or shaping using a variety of techniques and stitches simultaneously.

Yarn Weight Symbol & Names	LACE 0	SUPER FINE 1	FINE 2	LIGHT 3	MEDIUM 4	BULKY 5	SUPER BULKY 6	JUMBO 7
Type of Yarns in Category	Fingering, size 10 crochet thread	Sock, Fingering, Baby	Sport, Baby	DK, Light Worsted	Worsted, Afghan, Aran	Chunky, Craft, Rug	Super Bulky, Roving	Jumbo, Roving
Knit Gauge Ranges in Stockinette St to 4" (10 cm)	33-40 sts**	27-32 sts	23-26 sts	21-24 sts	16-20 sts	12-15 sts	7-11 sts	6 sts and fewer
Advised Needle Size Range	000 to 1	1 to 3	3 to 5	5 to 7	7 to 9	9 to11	11 to 17	17 and larger

* GUIDELINES ONLY: The chart above reflects the most commonly used gauges and needle sizes for specific yarn categories.

** Lace weight yarns are usually knitted on larger needles to create lacy openwork patterns. Accordingly, a gauge range is difficult to determine. Always follow the gauge stated in your pattern.

SYMBOLS & TERMS

( ) or [ ] — contains explanatory remarks.

GAUGE

Exact gauge is **essential** for proper size. Before beginning your project, make a sample swatch in the yarn and needle specified in the individual instructions. After completing the swatch, measure it, counting your stitches and rows or rounds carefully. If your swatch is larger or smaller than specified, **make another, changing needle size to get the correct gauge**. Keep trying until you find the size needle(s) that will give you the specified gauge.

MARKERS

As a convenience to you, we have used markers to help distinguish the beginning of a round or for placement. Place markers as instructed. You may use purchased markers or tie a length of contrasting color yarn around the needle. When you reach a marker on each round, slip it from the left needle to the right needle; remove it when no longer needed.

When using double pointed needles, a split-ring marker can be placed around the first stitch in the round to indicate the beginning of the round. Move it up as the first stitch of each round is worked.

KNITTING IN THE ROUND

Circular Needle

When you knit a tube, you are going to work around on the outside of the circle, with the **right** side of the knitting facing you.

Using a circular needle, cast on all stitches as instructed. Untwist and straighten the stitches on the needle to be sure that the cast on ridge lays on the inside of the needle and never rolls around the needle.

Hold the needle so that the ball of yarn is attached to the stitch closest to the **right** hand point. Place a marker on the right hand point to mark the beginning of the round.

To begin working in the round, knit the stitches on the left hand point **(Fig. 1)**.

Fig. 1

Double Pointed Needles

When working too few stitches to use a circular needle, double pointed needles are required. Divide the stitches between three double pointed needles **(Fig. 2a)**. Being careful not to twist the cast on ridge, form a triangle with the needles. With the remaining needle, knit across the stitches on the first needle **(Fig. 2b)**. You will now have an empty needle with which to knit the stitches from the next needle. Work the first stitch of each needle firmly to prevent gaps.

Fig. 2a

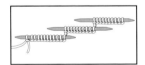

Fig. 2b

INCREASES

Knit In Front & Back
(abbreviated kfb)

Knit the next stitch but do **not** slip the old stitch off the left needle **(Fig. 3a)**. Insert the right needle into the **back** loop of the **same** stitch and knit it **(Fig. 3b)**, then slip the old stitch off the left needle.

Fig. 3a

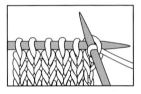

Fig. 3b

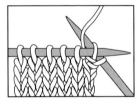

Yarn Over
(abbreviated YO)
Bring the yarn forward **between** the needles, then back **over** the top of the right hand needle, so that it is now in position to knit the next stitch **(Fig. 4)**.

Fig. 4

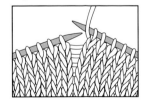

Make One
(abbreviated M1)

Insert the **left** needle under the horizontal strand between the stitches from the **front** *(Fig. 5a)*, then knit into the **back** of the strand *(Fig. 5b)*.

Fig. 5a

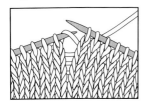

Fig. 5b

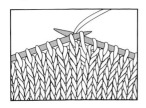

DECREASES

Knit 2 Together
(abbreviated K2 tog)

Insert the right needle into the **front** of the first two stitches on the left needle as if to **knit** *(Fig. 6)*, then **knit** them together as if they were one stitch.

Fig. 6

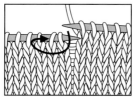

Purl 2 Together
(abbreviated P2 tog)

Insert the right needle into the **front** of the first two stitches on the left needle as if to **purl** *(Fig. 7)*, then **purl** them together as if they were one stitch.

Fig. 7

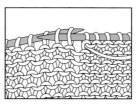

Slip, Slip, Knit
(abbreviated SSK)

Separately slip two stitches as if to **knit** *(Fig. 8a)*. Insert the **left** needle into the **front** of both slipped stitches *(Fig. 8b)* and **knit** them together as if they were one stitch *(Fig. 8c)*.

Fig. 8a

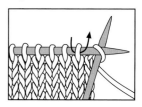

Fig. 8b

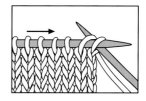

Fig. 8c

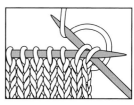

Knit 3 Together
(abbreviated K3 tog)

Insert the right needle into the **front** of the first three stitches on the left needle as if to **knit** *(Fig. 9)*, then **knit** them together as if they were one stitch.

Fig. 9

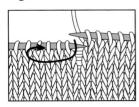

PICKING UP STITCHES

When instructed to pick up stitches, insert the needle from the **front** to the **back** under two strands at the edge of the worked piece *(Figs. 10a & b)*. Put the yarn around the needle as if to **knit**, then bring the needle with the yarn back through the stitch to the right side, resulting in a stitch on the needle.

Repeat this along the edge, picking up the required number of stitches.

A crochet hook may be helpful to pull yarn through.

Fig. 10a

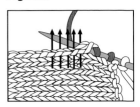

Fig. 10b

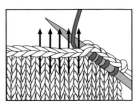

Made in U.S.A.

We have made every effort to ensure that these instructions are accurate and complete. We cannot, however, be responsible for human error, typographical mistakes, or variations in individual work.

Copyright © 2019 by Leisure Arts, Inc., 104 Champs Blvd., STE 100, Maumelle, AR 72113-6738, www.leisurearts.com. All rights reserved. This publication is protected under federal copyright laws. Reproduction or distribution of this publication or any other Leisure Arts publication, including publications which are out of print, is prohibited unless specifically authorized. This includes, but is not limited to, any form of reproduction or distribution on or through the Internet, including posting, scanning, or e-mail transmission.